REMEMBERING OUR BLACK TRAILBLAZERS AND THEIR LEGACIES II

Barbara A. Pierce

Remembering Our Black Trailblazers and Their Legacies II by Barbara A. Pierce

This book is written to provide information and motivation to readers. Its purpose is not to render any type of psychological, legal, or professional advice of any kind. The content is the sole opinion and expression of the author, and not necessarily that of the publisher.

Copyright © 2018 by Barbara A. Pierce

All rights reserved. No part of this book may be reproduced, transmitted, or distributed in any form by any means, including, but not limited to, recording, photocopying, or taking screenshots of parts of the book, without prior written permission from the author or the publisher. Brief quotations for noncommercial purposes, such as book reviews, permitted by Fair Use of the U.S. Copyright Law, are allowed without written permissions, as long as such quotations do not cause damage to the book's commercial value. For permissions, write to the publisher, whose address is stated below.

Printed in the United States of America.

New Leaf Media, LLC
175 S. 3rd Street, Suite 200
Columbus, OH 43215
www.thenewleafmedia.com

DEDICATION AND ACKNOWLEDGEMENTS

This book is dedicated to those whose mission in life has been to help others.
Thanks again to Barry Coleman for letting me access his
technical knowledge to complete this project.
And thanks to all of those who have continued to support my efforts.

All images are from Wikipedia's public domain African American historical pictures.

REMEMBERING OUR BLACK TRAILBLAZER AND THEIR LEGACIES II

TABLE OF CONTENTS

Introduction			1
Oscar Micheaux	1884 1951	Filmmaker, Author	3
Shirley Chisholm	1924 2005	Educator, Politician	5
Norbert Rillieux	1806 1894	Inventor	7
Guion Stewart Bluford, Jr.	1942	Astronaut	9
Frederick McKinley Jones	1893 1961	Inventor	11
Hank Aaron	1934	Baseball Player	13
Zora Neale Hurston	1891 1960	Writer	15
Mary Ann Shadd Cary	1823 1893	News Paper Woman, Lawyer	17
Angella D. Ferguson	1925	Physician (first to diagnose sickle cell disease)	19
Charles Clinton Spaulding	1849 1952	Business Leader	21
Arthur A. Schomburg	1874 1938	Collector of African American History	23
Ralph Bunche	1904 1971	Won Nobel Peace Prize	25
Arthur Robert Ashe	1943 1993	Tennis Player	27
William E. Burghardt Du Bois	1868 1963	Writer, Civil Right Advocate	29
Fannie Lou Hamer	1917 1977	Civil Rights Activist	31
Benjamin O. Davis Sr.	1880 1970	First African American General	33
Maggie Lena Walker	1864 1934	Educator, Businesswoman	35
James Weldon Johnson	1871 1938	Educator, Writer, Musician	37
Dorothy Irene Height	1912 2010	Headed Women's Organizations	39

Nat King Cole	1919 1965	Musician, Singer..........................41
Katherine Coleman Johnson	1918	Research Mathematician for NASA....43
Paul R. Williams	1894 1980	Architect 45
Mae Carol Jemison	1956	Physician, Astronaut......................47
Louis Daniel Armstrong	1901 1971	Jazz Musician, Singer.....................49
Barbara Charlaine Jordan	1936 1996	Lawyer, Politician 51
John H. Johnson	1918 2005	Publisher, Philanthropist 53
Wilt Chamberlain	1936 1999	Basketball Player 55
Alex Haley	1921 1992	Author 57
Patricia Bath	1942	Ophthalmologist, Inventor............59
Hattie McDaniel	1895 1952	Radio and TV Entertainer, Film Star 61
William Grant Still	1895 1978	Composer, Symphony Orchestra Conductor 63
Lawrence Douglas Wilder	1931	First African American Governor..65
Lloyd Augustus Hall	1894 1971	Scientist, Food Chemist 67
Alexa Canady	1950	Pediatric Neurosurgeon 69

Bibliography..71

Additional Research Recommendations...73

INTRODUCTION

Remembering Our Black Trailblazers and Their Legacies II, is the second book of the series. Just as in the first, it includes thirty-four brilliant African American men and woman who are trailblazers. They had big dreams and made great sacrifices to accomplish them. Their contributions were not just beneficial for themselves or their race of people, but for the whole of humanity. While each entry is a brief biographical sketch, the author hopes readers will be inspired to want to know more about each trailblazer's life story, then do a little research. Though the biographies appearing in this book are limited in number, there are still great numbers of unsung heroes remaining. At the end of the book are additional names recommended to be researched.

Inspirational saying by Langston Hughes:

"Hold fast to dreams,
for if dreams die,
life is a broken-winged bird
that can not fly."

Oscar Micheaux
Born: 1884
Died: 1951

OSCAR MICHEAUX

Oscar Micheaux is reported to be America's first Black filmmaker. Born on a farm in Metropolis, Illinois in 1884 to Calvin and Belle, he was the fifth of their thirteen children. The family later moved to a bigger city in search of a better education system for the children. The Micheauxs enjoyed a bit of prosperity for a number of years before they met with financial difficulties and had to relocate again, but this time back to the farm. The move caused such rebellion from Oscar, his father sent him away to work in Chicago. There he worked at such jobs as coal miner, longshoreman, Pullman porter, among others. The time away from the family and having to fend for himself, proved to be a real informal education for Oscar. He developed needed social skills and became economically stable. His traveling gave him the opportunity to connect with important contacts who later would become supporters in his future. Due to his thriftiness with his earnings, he was able to move to Gregory, South Dakota in 1913 to homestead. By age twenty-four Oscar purchased several acres of prairie land on the Rosebud Indian Reservation to build a house and barn. He later became interested in writing his first novel, The Conquest: The Story of a Negro Pioneer, and published it. He sold twenty-five hundred copies by soliciting door to door. When the owners of the Lincoln Motion Picture Company of California suggested Oscar let them adapt his novel to film, he accepted the offer. But when they refused to let him direct it, he started his own company in Chicago and produced it himself. Then he could be certain the prevailing stereotypical negative depictions of black life during that era were not perpetuated. As a teen he had witnessed too many scenes of that nature. His intent was to counter such stereotypes and dramatize the human need of social acceptance and assimilation. The self-made pioneer wrote seven novels and produced forty-four films. His films often caused much controversy because they explored the strained relationship between the races in the American culture. Oscar Micheaux died March 25, 1951. Awards in his honor are given to talented young African American filmmakers annually by The Black Filmmakers' Hall of Fame.

Shirley Chisholm
Born: 1924
Died: 2005

SHIRLEY CHISHOLM

Shirley Chisholm was born November 30, 1924 in Brooklyn, New York to Charles St. Hill and Ruby Seale. she was the eldest of three other sisters. After her fifth birthday, the children were sent to live with their grandmother on her farm in Christ Church, Barbados. Shirley wrote in her 1970 autobiography "Unbought and Unbossed", years later how grateful she was for the experience of being raised in such an environment where she received a strict, traditional, British-style education. She attributes her ability to speak and write well to that disciplined upbringing. She let it be known in the book that her grandmother's influence in her early years made her strong and confident. She writes "Granny gave me strength, dignity, and love. I learned from an early age that I was somebody. I didn't need the black revolution to tell me that." Upon completing her education in the New York State, Shirley worked as an educator until she became interested in politics. She began working as a volunteer for white dominated political clubs and the League of Women Voters in Bedford-Stuyvesant. Eventually, Chisholm's success leads her to be elected in 1968 as the Democratic National Committeewoman from New York, then she became the first African-American woman to be elected to the United States Congress. She was also the first Black candidate for a major political party's nomination for President of the United States. In 1972, she was the Democratic Party's presidential nominee. It is believed that because her campaign was poorly organized and funded she was not considered a serious political figure. Shirley felt that she did not get the full support of the entire Democratic political establishment, nor from her Black male colleagues. Though she was not successful in her bid to become the President of the United States, her political career did not end there. When Shirley did finally retire from politics, she returned to her career in education. She died on January 1, 2005 at 80 years old.

Norbert Rillieux
Born: 1806
Died: 1894

NORBERT RILLIEUX

Norbert Rillieux was an inventor who developed a new way to change the juice of sugar cane into sugar. He was the off-spring of a French immigrant plantation owner and a free mulatto woman. The boy was born March 17, 1806 on his father's cane plantation in New Orleans. As the boy grew older, he began questioning his dad about how the mechanisms of his farm machinery worked. When his father recognized his son's ability to grasp the intricate details, he was quite impressed. However, when he tried to enroll Norbert in the best of New Orleans schools, he was refused admittance because of his race. The boy was then sent to study mechanical engineering at L'Ecole Centrale in Paris, France. His exceptional academic performance resulted in him becoming part of the school's faculty as a teacher after graduation. He was the youngest teacher ever hired there. Also, his vast knowledge of machinery and additional study in sugar refining prepared him to play a big role in the Industrial Revolution that was taking place in Paris at the time. He did research and wrote about the new steam engines that were being used around the world. Upon his return to New Orleans, Norbert found the sugar-refining process unchanged, still the same as before, slow, dangerous, and antiquated. A dark crude form of sugar resembling molasses was still the result of that process. Growing up on his father's plantation, Norbert had witnessed the hardship facing the slaves to make sugar. They poured large vats of boiling hot sugarcane juice repeatedly from one vessel into another to increase the evaporation of the liquid. The process became known as the "Jamaica Train". Norbert Rillieux put an end to the "Jamaica Train" process when he designed a new steam engine evaporator that worked faster and cheaper. And the quality of sugar was better also. The machine was used to produce other products needed as well. Norbert Rillieux filed his patent on August 26, 1843. He died October 8, 1894 in Paris, France.

Guion Stewart Bluford, Jr.
Born: 1942

GUION STEWART BLUFORD, JR.

Guion Stewart Bluford, Jr. was born in Philadelphia, Pennsylvania on November 22, 1942. His parents were Guion Sr. a mechanical engineer and Lolita a teacher. Guion Jr. was the eldest of three boys. Guion, Jr. followed his dream of becoming an astronaut. He was the first African-American to ever go on a mission with a crew into outer space. The suggestion that he was not college material by his high school counselor fueled his determination to succeed academically. Guion Jr. refused to settle for the counselor's predicted path for his future. Attending college became a priority for him. After graduation, he was accepted in the aerospace engineering program at Pennsylvania State University. He spent much of his time studying and taking an active role in the Reserve Officers' Training Corps (ROTC). At graduation in 1964 he received a B.A. degree in aerospace engineering from Pennsylvania State University. He also graduated as a distinguished Air Force ROTC graduate. Afterwards, joining the Air Force provided him with the opportunity to become a pilot. Guion earned his wings in 1965. When there came a demand for the best pilots during the Vietnam War he joined the F-4C fighter squadron based in Cam Ranh Bay in South Vietnam. He served with the 557th Tactical Fighter Squadron. His phantom jet made 144 combat missions, that includes 65 over North Vietnam. His logged 3,000 hours of flying time qualified him as a military hero. Many medals were given Guion for his heroic deeds. In 1974 the scientist received a Master's of Science degree from the Air Force Institute of Technology. In 1978, he receives a Doctorate in aerospace engineering with a minor in laser physics. At the end of 1978, he was accepted as one out of over eighty-eight hundred applicants for thirty-five spots to become an astronaut with NASA. Guion Stewart Bluford finally realizes his childhood dream.

Frederick McKinley Jones
Born: 1893
Died: 1961

FREDERICK MCKINLEY JONES

Frederick McKinley Jones a self-taught inventor was born in Cincinnati, Ohio. After the death of his mother, Jones was raised by his father. However, at the passing of his father, Jones then nine, was sent to live in a Kentucky rectory under the direction of Father Ryan. There the boy attended school and did odd jobs. At the age sixteen, Jones set out on his own to look for employment. In his travels he became so taken with the advent of new automobiles, he'd seize every opportunity to check the mechanical parts and their functions under the hood of the machines. Though lacking in much formal education, he did have the ability to understand machinery. Taking a risk, Jones accepted a job as a mechanic. He was a willing worker, one with no quarrel against hard work, or getting his hands dirty. If a difficult problem arose with the machinery that required concern, he visited the library to study books on the subject, a habit that he maintained during his lifetime. Jones did prove himself to his new employer. Through the years, Jones' jobs and adventures were many. Enlisting in the Army during World War I, Jones served as an electrician in France. For his service he earned the rank of sergeant. Upon his return to the States at nineteen, Jones tried his hand at the art of car racing until he had a near fatal accident. He accepted an offer as a mechanic in 1912 to keep machinery on a 50,000-acre Minnesota farm in good repair. He spent eighteen years learning and working in that environment. Jones' vivid imagination turned to the science of sound related to the radio and the movie industry's soundtrack. However, in the late 1930s Jones started designing portable air coolers for trucks to prevent perishable food spoilage. Not long after that he invented the first truck air condition. His cooling units were very important to the American Military in World War II to maintain the proper temperatures of blood for transfusions, and for medicines. Jones was awarded more than 60 patents before his death in 1961. Forty of his patents were related to refrigeration equipment and the rest were for other inventions.

Hank Aaron
Born: 1934

HANK AARON

Hank Aaron whose birth name is actually Henry Louis Aaron, was one of America's most accomplished baseball players. He was born in Mobile, Alabama in 1934 to Herbert Aaron, Sr. and Estella Aaron. Hank was one of their eight children. He started playing baseball early in his childhood. Because the family could not afford any baseball equipment, he and his brother used sticks to hit bottle tops in a cleared pecan grove beside their home. Much later when the city initiated a recreational league for the black youths, Hank joined. In his high school years, he played outfield and third base for the Mobile Bears a semi-pro team. It was not too long before his powerful batting skills were noticed. Hank had his first tryout for the Major League team, the Brooklyn Dodgers at age fifteen in 1949. When Aaron failed to make it, he returned to school. In 1951 he signed with the Indianapolis Clowns of the Negro American League. Months later, Hank received offers via telegrams from the New York Giants and the Boston Braves (Known later as the Atlanta Braves). The Howe Sports Bureau credits Hank with a .366 batting average in 26 official Negro League games, with 5 home runs, 33 runs batted in (RBI), 41 hits, and 9 stolen bases, before leaving the Indianapolis Clowns. Hank signed a contract with the Boston Braves June 12, 1952. Hank Aaron's career lasted twenty-three years in the major leagues. His total for runs batted in is 2,297. And for three consecutive years (1958, 1959 and 1960) he was a Gold Glove Winner. At forty in 1974, Hank made a 385-foot home run while playing against the Los Angeles Dodgers. He passed Babe Ruth's record of 714 career home runs. Hank set a new record of 755, surpassing all home run records. Though Hank was aware between 1972 and 1974 the closer he came to Babe Ruth's record there was serious discontentment among a segment of the white population. Despite the hate mail and death threats that required FBI involvement, he neither held back or backed down from his dream. Hank Aaron let it be known he didn't want Babe Ruth's fans to forget him, but he wanted to be remembered as well. Hank Aaron has accomplished much more than being one of the greatest baseball players, he has done other things too. After retiring in 1976, he founded the Hank Aaron Rookie League program and he returned to the Braves as a vice president. In 1982 he was inducted into the National Baseball Hall of Fame.

Zora Neale Hurston
Born: 1891
Died: 1960

ZORA NEALE HURSTON

Zora Neale Hurston was a popular Black American writer and anthropologist in the twentieth century. Her literary work was well received for twenty years before actually going out of print. Nevertheless, small but very devoted readers continued to keep her literature relevant. Today, there is an active resurgence of Hurston's literary legacy because of its importance to African-American and women's literature. Zora was born on January 7, 1891 to John and Lucy Ann Hurston. She had six siblings. The family moved from Notasulga, Alabama to Eatonville, Florida where she was raised until her mother's death. When her father remarried, she was sent to live with a series of other relatives. Deciding to move to Baltimore, Maryland, Zora enrolled in Morgan College prep school until 1918. Then at Howard University she studied writing from 1919 until 1924. Zora won second prize in 1925, after entering her short story "Spunk" that appeared in Alain Locke's germinal anthology, The New Negro. She enrolled at Barnard College where she studied anthropology and earned a B.A. in 1928. Then enrolling in Colombia University's graduate anthropology program, Zora began to collect black folklore throughout the South and the Caribbean. While her work was well received, it was her fiction that got the most attention. Hurston's work included four novels: Jonah's Gourd Vine-1934, Their Eyes Were Watching God-1937, Moses, Man of the Mountain-1939, and Seraph on the Suwanee-1948----two books of folklore: Mules and Men-1935, and Tell My Horse-1938---an autobiography: Dust Tracks on a Road-1942, and over fifty short stories, essays and plays. Her experiences growing up in Eatonville later became the basis for shaping her views in her literature. She was one of the most widely read black authors between 1925 and 1945. Hurston is the very first novelist to depict a black woman's successful quest to find a voice and to overcome male oppression. However, there were a few prominent black male writers who thought of her writings as problematic during that era. Zora Neale Hurston died in 1960.

Mary Ann Shadd Cary
Born: 1823
Died: 1893

MARY ANN SHADD CARY

Mary Ann Shadd Cary was born to parents who were known anti-slavery activists. As activists they avail themselves to any slave secretly seeking freedom. Of course, Mary Ann witnessing the frequent visits of traveling slaves seeking refuge in the Shadds' home strongly impacted her views and actions later in her adult life. When the family moved from Delaware to West Chester, Pennsylvania Mary Ann, the oldest of the Shadd children, was ten years old. Since Pennsylvania was not a slave state, the Shadd children could legally attend school. They received their education from Quakers who felt that slavery was immoral and wrong. Compelled to follow God's law rather than man's, they believed that all human beings were entitled to their God given freedom. When Quakers used the terms "thee" and "thou" addressing individuals instead of "you" was their way of showing respect for all. Mary Ann proved to be an excellent student under the guidance of the Quakers. Along with the usual subjects of math, literature, and writing, she studied philosophy and languages. After graduating at sixteen, Mary Ann became a teacher to other African-Americans. She also took an active role in some of the activists' activities of her parents. Eventually, the Shadds joined with the Quakers in their activities involving the Underground Railroad, a secretly organized group of people who worked together to help the slaves in their escape to freedom. However, a big change came September 18, 1850 when Congress passed the Fugitive Slave Act. Slaves could be hunted down anywhere in the U.S. and taken back to their slave masters. This posed a real danger for the family even though they were legally free. The law did not prevent the kidnapping of free African-Americans by whites. In 1852, Mary Ann found refuge in Winsor, Ontario, Canada. Her family soon joined her. She published the weekly Canadian newspaper The Provincial Freeman to encouraged African-Americans to move to Canada where they could live safely. She resumed her teaching career and took on the role as spokesperson to expose the horrid injustices plaguing the United States. Mary Ann even joined in the early women's suffrage movement. (Suffrage refers to women's right to vote.) In later years she graduated law school. After passing the bar, Mary Ann Shadd Cary was the first black female to become an attorney in the U.S. Her focus was women's rights. She accomplished many significant things before her death in 1893.

Angella D. Ferguson
Born: 1925

ANGELLA D. FERGUSON

Angella D. Ferguson a trailblazer in medicine, was born in Washington, D.C., February 15, 1925. She was one of eight siblings. Though family suffered economically as most black families did in the 1920s, her parents stressed the importance of getting an education. They believed education was necessary for a productive life and a buffer to discrimination and oppression. Early in elementary school, Angella was recognized as talented and a leader. She was a voracious reader and always wanted to know more. She always made the honor. In high school Angella loved chemistry. Her teacher at Cardoso seemed to make science come alive for her. After graduating at the top of her class in 1941, she took a job as a secretary briefly, then entered Howard University to pursue medicine. While at Howard, she became interested in anatomy and physiology. After receiving a bachelor of science, Angella was accepted in Howard's School of Medicine. So, few black females were in medical school, Angella knew she'd have to be smarter than her male colleagues to get respect. As a medical student Angella was assigned to cover many wards at Freedmen's Hospital. Her compassion for the many sick children there motivated her choice to enter a two-year training program in pediatrics. After passing all medical board requirements, Dr. Ferguson set up her private pediatrics practice in Washington. Aware at the time, that minimal research existed about the health of African American children, she set out to do her own. She knew the research that did exist was based on children of European decent, thus the results would not reveal accurately the needs for African American children. She had studied hundreds of patients with the sickle cell disease that showed certain symptoms. Healthy red blood cells are donut shaped, but blood cells of sickle cell patients are in sickle shapes and causes great distress because the misshapen cells often get stuck in the blood vessels, preventing the flow of blood and oxygen. She observed that blood of those patients were much thicker and had a higher acidic content than the blood of her healthy patients. From her findings she was able to devise an innovative way to diagnose the disease. Today, just about every state is required to test newborns for the disease. Because of pioneers like Dr. Ferguson more scientists are trying to find ways to prevent a sickle cell crisis from happening at all.

Charles Clinton Spaulding
Born: 1849
Died: 1952

CHARLES CLINTON SPAULDING

Charles Clinton Spaulding was a leading African-American insurance and banking executive in the 1900s. His parents Benjamin Spaulding Sr. and Margaret Moore were farmers in Columbus, County, North Carolina where he was born in 1849. Charles was one of their fourteen children. Though the schooling for Blacks was limited, Charles was eager to learn. He read and studied whatever was available to him. Despite the poor education he received, Spaulding's dreams went beyond that of the Columbus County farm, his native home. Leaving the farming life, the boy relocated to small town Durham, North Carolina where he accepted a job as a dishwasher to support himself. A series of other menial jobs followed which he saw as a stepping-stone to a promising future. When he had saved enough of his meager earnings, Charles Spaulding satisfied one of his greatest desires. He enrolled in the Durham public schools. After graduating in 1898, he was chosen to run a newly formed black-owned grocery cooperative. When its original supporters lost interest, Spaulding was forced to assume full responsibility alone. The business became profitable, but it remained quite small. The young man was unaware he was being observed during the hold ordeal. So, impressed with Spaulding's foresight and business integrity, he was asked by seven black entrepreneurs, including his uncle with whom he lived, to join them in a new business venture. Since they were the founders of North Carolina Mutual, neither had the time to run the new company. So, Charles Spaulding was hired to run it. Once he came aboard the company's network and operations expanded quickly. In 1919, he used his influence to restructure the company. And that same year it was renamed the North Carolina Mutual Life Insurance Company. Soon after, it began operating in thirteen states and the District of Columbia. In 1923 Spaulding was made president. During his lifetime he took an active role in civic progress. In 1926 he was awarded the Harmon Foundation Gold Medal for distinguished achievement in business. Charles Clinton Spaulding died August 1, 1952 at the age of 78 in Durham, North Carolina. It is said he lived by his favorite motto: "Success is carved out by the chisel of efficiency, integrity, and hard work."

Arthur A. Schomburg
Born: 1874
Died: 1938

ARTHUR A. SCHOMBURG

Arthur A. Schomburg was the foremost nineteen century collector of books, prints, manuscripts, and pictures relating to the African-American culture. His interest began very early in his childhood once he became aware that differences were made in the treatment of the races. Schomburg observed that the best of everything was reserved for whites or near-whites while blacks received less. He was prompted to research black history more vigorously when his white classmates insisted that blacks had not really accomplished anything significant and never would. On such occasions, armed with new knowledge he was able to refute the uninformed claims with solid facts. Schomburg was born in San Juan, Puerto Rico. He attended school there and also in the Danish West Indies. His experiences on both islands fueled his enthusiasm to collect books and facts about African-American history. In 1901 Schomburg immigrated to New York City where he was employed as a law clerk. Also, during that time, he was an active member of a movement to gain Cuban and Puerto independence. After Cuba won its independence he left on a scientific expedition to Central America and Haiti. Once back in the states, Schomburg was hired by the Bankers Trust Company of Wall Street. There he spent the bulk of his free time on his hobby, collecting and writing. He was also instrumental in the founding of the Negro Society for Historical Research. And in 1892 he was elected president of the American Negro Academy. In 1924 he traveled to Europe where he made important discoveries that threw new light on Negro History. One eye opener from his visit and research is the fact that American slavery originated in the Iberian Peninsula. His visit to Spain revealed that Juan Pareja and Sebastian Gomez, two of their noted painters were definitely Blacks. And on his visit to France, Germany, England, and other countries more important discoveries to add to his collection were made. Arthur A. Schomburg retired from the bank in 1929 to become the curator at Fisk University.

Ralph Bunche
Born: 1904
Died: 1971

RALPH BUNCHE

Ralph Bunche was born in Detroit, Michigan on August 7, 1904. His family was very poor. At an early age Ralph had to deliver newspapers to help his family with their finances. When the boy was eleven he lost both his mother and father due to illness. Ralph and his grandmother moved to Los Angeles, California, where the grandmother was able to get employment. Ralph was now not expected to work. His grandmother insisted he focus on his studies. And he did not disappoint her. The boy received awards in History and in English at the end of elementary school. And also, in 1922, he was awarded medals at his high school graduation for his work in civics and debating. After graduation Ralph thought he should get a job to support his grandmother, but she insisted he attend college. So, he enrolled at the University of California in Los Angeles after getting a four-year athletic scholarship. To help with additional expenditures Ralph signed on as a janitor for the college gym. In 1927 Ralph Bunche was graduated Summa Cum Laude from the University. And because of his hard work, he was the class valedictorian and elected to Phi Beta Kappa. He also received five medals for his outstanding academics and a scholarship to attend Harvard University. Thousands of dollars were collected by his neighbors to help with his expenses at Harvard. Without warning Ralph's grandmother passed away just a few days before he was to leave for graduate school. Distraught over her death, Ralph considered not going away, but knowing how hard she had worked to give him an education, she would be pleased if he went. In 1928, Ralph Bunche graduated from Harvard with a Master's of Arts Degree in Political Science, and accepted an opening at Howard University. In 1930, Bunche received a scholarship from Harvard which allowed him to begin work on a doctorate. After receiving the Rosenwald Fellowship in 1931 he did a year of travel and study through Europe and Africa doing research on various social problems for his doctorate. He received it from Harvard in 1934. A recognized authority on race relations in the States, Bunche was given a leave to study race relations between people in the U.S.A. From his study he wrote his book, An America Dilemma. In 1947 Bunche responded to the United Nations request of him to act as a mediator to try to establish peace between the Arabs and the Jews. In 1950, he was awarded the Nobel Peace Prize.

Arthur Robert Ashe
Born: 1943
Died: 1993

ARTHUR ROBERT ASHE

Arthur R. Ashe was a trailblazer in the sport of tennis, a sport once thought to be for the white elite only. In 1963, that changed with Ashe being the first black player selected to the United States Davis Cup team. He was the only black ever to win the singles title at Wimbledon, the U.S. Open, and the Australian Open. In 1968 and 1975 he was ranked number one in the world by The Daily Telegraph and the World Tennis Magazine. He was born on July 10, 1943 to Arthur Ashe, Sr. and Mattie C. Ashe. When Mattie died in 1950, Arthur and his younger brother were raised by their father. At the tender age of seven young Arthur was not only encouraged to excel in school, but to try sports, tennis preferably. American football, the popular game of many black children was forbidden by his father because of the boy's slight build. Young Arthur's talent was discovered as he practiced tennis at a blacks-only public playground in Richmond, Virginia near his home. Virginia Union University student and tennis instructor, Ron Charity, the best black player in town at the time, taught him some basic strokes and suggested he enter local tournaments. Ashe continued to practice tennis through Maggie L. Walker High School. Ron Charity introduced the boy to Robert Walter Johnson who agreed to coach and mentor Ashe at his tennis summer camp home in Lynchburg, Virginia from 1953 to 1960. Johnson's intent was to fine-tune the boy's game and to teach him the importance of racial socialization through sportsmanship, etiquette and composure. In 1958, Ashe participated in his first integrated tennis competition. He was the first Black American to play in the Maryland boys' championships. But in the final year of high school he's not allowed in competition during the school year, nor was the city's inside courts open to black players. So, Ashe accepts the offer to move to St. Louis with a tennis coach and his family for a year. His coach helped him develop the serve-and-volley game his body was able to handle since he was now stronger. In 1961, after some lobbying by his previous coach, Dr. Johnson, Arthur Ashe was given permission to participate in the once segregated U.S. Interscholastic Tournament and won it for his school. Ashe was featured in Sports Illustrated in December 1960 and again in 1963. He was the first African American to win the National Junior Indoor tennis title. Though Arthur Ashe became quite famous, he used his celebrity status along the way to draw attention to the moral inequalities in this society.

William E. Burghardt Du Bois
Born: 1868
Died: 1963

WILLIAM E. BURGHARDT DU BOIS

William E. Du Bois was one of the most influential African-Americans of the twentieth century. He was born on February 23, 1868 in Great Barrington, Massachusetts. His father left the family a year after his birth. While the family was left poor, their social and educational standards were set higher than that of average black families of that time. Du Bois exhibited remarkable intelligence from his youth. He was the first African-American to graduate from his high school in 1884. During the graduation he received high honors. Du Bois wanted to attend Harvard after high school, but when his mother died he was without funds. The local white leaders from Congregational churches gave him a scholarship to Fisk University. Though disappointed he was not going to the university of his choice, he saw an opportunity to learn something about the black experience in the South. Du Bois' years at Fisk revealed the social conditions among Blacks in that city. For the first time in his life he found himself on intimate terms with black poverty and suffering as was evident when he spent summers teaching in the rural South. Experiences such as those were instrumental in developing his social and cultural consciousness. After graduating from Fisk in 1888, Du Bois enrolled at Harvard. He became the first African-American to earn a Ph. D in the history of Harvard. Later, funded on an American fellowship he studied economics and sociology at the University of Berlin. The Suppression of the African Slave Trade to the United States of America, 1638—1870 published in 1896, and The Philadelphia Negro in 1899 were the first works of scientific importance on Blacks by an African-American. Between 1897 and 1903 Du Bois was one of the most prolific writers in the nation. Later, he became one of the most active co-founders of The National Association for the Advancement of Colored People (NAACP). And as the editor of that organization's official magazine, the Crisis, Du Bois was a champion of Negro rights. He died at the age of ninety-four in Ghana, West Africa in 1963. Some of his other works are, Color and Democracy, The American Negro Family, Gift of Black Folk, Black Reconstruction, Black Folk Then and Now, Dusk of Dawn, and Souls of Black Folk.

Fannie Lou Hamer
Born: 1917
Died: 1977

FANNIE LOU HAMER

Fannie Lou Hamer became a voice for the civil-rights movement in the South. Though she had only a limited education, Fannie represented herself and her fellow African-Americans in the fight for economic, social, and political equality. Her valiant fight to become a delegate to the national Democratic Party was effective enough that she became one of the party's first black delegates to a presidential convention. Fannie Lou Hamer was the youngest of twenty siblings. Her family made a meager living as sharecroppers. At the young age of six she was expected to work along with the other children. At twelve, she was taken out of school to be a full-time sharecropper in the fields of the white land owners. Such was her life until she married and moved with her husband in 1944. Fannie started going to the Student Nonviolent Coordinating Committee (SNCC), a group that encouraged blacks to exercise their rights as voters. Failing her first literacy test, a complex passage of the Mississippi state constitution, Fannie returned home to threats of eviction by her landlord of eighteen years. She was warned to stop attempting to register to vote. Even though she and her family left immediately, they were harassed continuously. She later indicated that being kicked off of the plantation, set her free. Fannie Lou continued preparing for her voter registration. And after being coached in constitutional interpretation by leaders in the organization like James Forman and Robert Moses, Fannie passed the literacy test. After accepting a job with the Council of Federated Organizations (COFO), Fannie recruits and trains others. Because of economic reprisals, intimidation and violence waged against Blacks for even attempting to register, her job was an extremely difficult one. The civil activities at times ended with Fannie and her colleagues arrested. On one such occasion Fannie received serious injuries while incarcerated. In 1964, she helped in the founding of the Mississippi Freedom Democratic party which brought in black and white volunteers to help educate and empower black voters. She then ran as a candidate for the U.S. Senate intent on forcing the state's white Democratic party open to black voters. That next year, President Lyndon B. Johnson signed the Voting Rights Act. Before Fannie Lou Hamer died in 1977, she was granted honorary degrees by Morehouse College and Howard University. She was also inducted as an honorary member of Delta Sigma Theta sorority.

Benjamin O. Davis Sr.
Born: 1880
Died: 1970

BENJAMIN O. DAVIS SR.

Benjamin O. Davis Sr. became the first Black general to serve in the United States Military. He was born in Washington, D.C. on May 28, 1880. His mother had aspirations of him becoming a minister, however he had a different career in mind. The youth was a good student and a talented athlete at the black M Street School in Washington. His frequent visits to watch the drill and arms presentations of an all-black cavalry stationed near-by, greatly influenced his career choice. Davis set his dream in motion when he joined the M Street High School's Cadet Corps. In his senior year he won a District of Columbia National Guard Commission. Davis was not sent into active duty as he had hoped, but was made first lieutenant of the Eighth United States Volunteer Infantry, Company G. It was an all-black newly organized unit. He experienced his first introduction to southern Jim Crow and racist segregation when he was stationed in one of Georgia's small towns. The following year in 1899, Davis enlisted as a clerk in Troop I, Ninth Cavalry and was sent to a desolate area in Utah. He spent some of his spare time teaching the illiterate veteran soldiers to read and write. He also spent time seeking an officer's commission in the regular army. In 1901 after Davis passed the grueling officer's test, he was discharged as an enlisted soldier and took his oath as a second lieutenant with the Tenth Cavalry. This time Davis was sent to the Philippines on a brief assignment during which time he learned to speak basic Spanish and Visayan. Shortly after, he and his unit were sent to Fort Washakie, Wyoming, another remote and empty land. Davis began to get it. He realized that despite the need for experienced officers like himself in World War l, he was put on hold to avoid a racial situation where he might have to command white troops or perhaps he might out rank a white officer. Along with his military duties, Davis continued to study and teach. It was not until 1937 he was put in charge of troops, the legendary 369th Infantry. Davis was promoted to a brigadier general by President Franklin D. Roosevelt in 1940, hoping to diminish the distrust blacks had of his administration and of the military. And in 1941 Davis was given the task of investigating race relations in the armed forces. Benjamin O. Davis retired in 1948 after fifty years of service and was awarded the Distinguished Medal for his work on the race question. Davis died in 1970. His son followed in his dad's footsteps. Benjamin O. Davis Jr. joined the military and became the first Black American general in the U.S. Navy.

Maggie Lena Walker
Born: 1864
Died: 1934

MAGGIE LENA WALKER

Maggie L. Walker was the first woman of any race to form a bank in the United States. She was born in Richmond, Virginia after the American Civil War on July 15, 1864. Her mother Elizabeth, a cook had been a former slave. Her father William Mitchell was a butler and a writer. After William's unexpected death, Elizabeth was left alone to support Maggie and her younger brother. She began taking in laundry from her church and school community since their home was near. Maggie helped her mother by delivering the clean clothes to the newly formed public schools. After Walker graduated from the public schools in Richmond, she taught elementary school three years before marrying Armstead Walker Jr. in 1886. Her husband earned a good living as a brick contractor, so Maggie was encouraged to leave teaching to take care of her family. She also had obligations to the Independent Order of St. Luke, a fraternal burial society started in Baltimore, Maryland in 1867. Its goal was to administer to the sick and aged, promote humanitarian causes, and encourage individual self-help and integrity. Maggie published a newspaper for the organization in 1902. And after serving in many capacities, she held top leadership position of Right Worthy Grand Secretary from 1888 until her death. Maggie made the bold move to form the St. Luke Penny Savings Bank in 1902, and served as its first president. Being the first Black to charter a bank in the United States and a woman at that, got a lot of attention. When her bank merged with two other banks she agreed to serve as chairman of the board of directors. The new bank became known as The Consolidated Bank and Trust Company, an African-American owned institution. When her husband was accidentally killed in 1902, it left Maggie with a big house and property to maintain. She and her family were still able to live quite comfortably because of her work and the wise investments she had made. Though Maggie Walker was stricken with a disability in her later years, she still nurtured the dream of improving the way of life for African-Americans and women. An honorary master's degree from Virginia Union University was received by Maggie Walker in 1925, and she was also inducted into the Junior Achievement U.S. Business Hall of Fame.

James Weldon Johnson
Born: 1871
Died: 1938

JAMES WELDON JOHNSON

James Weldon Johnson was born in Jacksonville, Florida on June 17, 1871. His father James worked as a headwaiter at a luxury hotel and his mother Helen was a school teacher. Coming from a middle-class family, he received an excellent education. His parents made sure he was given all of the educational opportunities available to him at the time. His mother taught him the piano. Later, he learned to write songs with his brother. His initial interest in becoming a doctor disappeared by the time he had graduated from Atlanta University in 1894. James Weldon chose to be principal of Stanton Elementary School in the Jacksonville school system. He eventually made it a high school because of the need for more high schools to accommodate black students. Stanton became only the fourth black high school in the entire South. While still the principal of Stanton, James studied law. He eventually left to form a legal partnership to become the first black lawyer admitted to the bar in Duval County, Florida. During his early years as a lawyer, James Weldon became active in the Republican Political Party. He was sent in 1906 as U.S. consul to Venezuela and in 1909 to Nicaragua. Upon his return in 1912 with a different political party in power, it was clear his chance of any political future was limited. That same year he published anonymously, his book, The Autobiography of an Ex- Colored Man. And in 1914 James Weldon took on the editorship of a prominent black newspaper the, New York Age. When he was assigned field organizer for the National Association for the Advancement of Colored People in its infancy in 1916, an explosive impact occurred. The organization's membership and reginal branches increased significantly. In 1920, James Weldon became secretary of the NAACP, an office he held for ten years. Later, he went to teach literature and writing at Fisk University. He published God's Trombones: Seven Sermons in Verse, The Book of American Negro Poetry, The Book of American Negro Spirituals, and The Second Book of American Negro Spirituals. As song writers James and his brother J. Rosamond Johnson are given credit for writing the adopted Negro national anthem "Lift Every Voice and Sing". James Weldon Johnson is known today as a key figure in the African-American literary tradition.

Dorothy Irene Height
Born: 1912
Died: 2010

DOROTHY IRENE HEIGHT

Dorothy I. Height was born on March 24, 1912, in Richmond, Virginia. She was quite young when her family move to the small mining town of Rankin, Pennsylvania. Her father was a building contractor and her mother was a nurse. She did well academically throughout her school years. Her orator skills were good enough to win the Elks Fraternal Society National Oratorical Competition. It allowed her to attend New York University and graduate with a bachelor's and a master's degree in psychology in 1933. She recognized there were particular problems adversely affecting low-income areas. Her reaction to that was to get involved in the local politics and become a caseworker for the New York City Welfare Department. And at the same time she took courses in social work to find out the means to counter the substandard conditions of black female domestic workers. Daily she witnessed many on the city streets while people in cars bargained for their housekeeping services. Height compared it to a modern slave market. Without adequate unionization, workers were poorly paid and often poorly treated. She took the issue of fair and equal payment to the New York City Council. That was her introduction as a labor union organizer. She waged a battle against black female labor exclusion, and influenced the formation of powerful black women's groups. Her spirited fight was not only for fair wages and union issues in the thirties and forties, it continued for civil rights and labor improvements in the sixties and seventies. And in the eighties and nineties she lobbied for black self-help programs for the extended family. After Mary McLeod Bethune's death in 1957, Dorothy Height became president of the National Council of Negro Women founded by Bethune in 1935.The Council was a coalition of thirty organizations representing four million women. Ms. Height was a recipient of many awards, however the most fitting was her being inducted into the International Women's Forum Hall of Fame in 1986. She died in 2010 at the age of 98.

Nat King Cole
Born: 1919
Died: 1965

NAT KING COLE

Nat King Cole was the first African-American artist to break into network television. He was born in Montgomery, Alabama on March 17, 1919 to Edward and Perlina Coles. His actual given name was Nathaniel Adams Coles. The family moved to Chicago, Illinois when Nat was four years old. His father became the minister of a Baptist church and his mother, the church organist. The boy was taught to play the organ by his mother, and by twelve he was singing and playing organ for his father. Nathaniel soon joined his brother's jazz band, the Rogues of Rhythm. He also took formal lessons where he played jazz, gospel, and Western classical music. He mastered musical compositions from Johann Sebastian Bach to Sergei Rachmaninoff. When the Coles family moved again to another area of Chicago, Nathaniel got the chance to listen to popular artists like Louis Armstrong and Earl Hines. He also got an opportunity to participate in the renowned musical program offered at DuSable High School conducted by Walter Dyett. Inspired by his favorite artists, Nathaniel changed his name in 1935, and embarked upon a career as a performing jazz pianist at sixteen. After touring for a year as a band director, Cole organized a small trio to perform at a Los Angeles night club. When the drummer dropped out, Cole became the band's vocalist. The band's biggest hits of the 1940s were "Sweet Lorraine", "Straighten Up and Fly Right", and "Get Your Kicks On Route 66". By the mid 1940s the name Nat King Cole was among the biggest names in jazz. In 1950, the songs "Mona Lisa", "Unforgettable", and "The Christmas Song" were his trademark numbers. Nat King Cole did not let any of the racism he encountered during that era cloud his path to success. He supported the civil rights movement, but he was unable to get support for his television show because he performed for segregated audiences. The show lasted just over a year. Nat King Cole will be remembered for his suave, velvet voice. He died on February 15, 1965 at the age of 45.

Katherine Coleman Johnson
Born: 1918

KATHERINE COLEMAN JOHNSON

Katherine Johnson was born in White Sulphur Springs, West Virginia on August 26, 1918. She was the youngest of four siblings. Very early Katherine exhibited signs of brilliance with numbers. Entering elementary school at four she did so well, by the time she turned ten in 1928, the child was ready for high school. With no high schools for blacks in her hometown, her parents had to make sacrifices to enroll her in a high school associated with West Virginia Collegiate Institute more than a hundred miles from White Sulphur Springs. She excelled at the new school. The teachers there sparked her interests in math and science as never before. In 1933, at the age of fifteen Katherine entered West Virginia State College (no longer West Virginia Collegiate Institute). Again, Katherine gains mentors who recognize her abilities. One professor in particular had the most impact in her later years. She suggested Katherine would make a good research mathematician. The girl did not have any idea how it related to her or what research mathematicians did. In 1937, Katherine graduates summa cum laude from college at the age of eighteen with a Mathematics and French degree. She starts a career teaching mathematics and French in West Virginia and later in Virginia. In 1952, when Katherine learned that the National Advisory Committee for Aeronautics (NACA) in Virginia was looking for women with skills in mathematics, she applied but was a bit too late that year. Refusing to give up, a year later she applied again and landed a job as a research mathematician at NACA. Experimenting with supersonic flight had just begun. There were no electronic computers to do the work, it had to be done the old-fashion way: with slide rules and mechanical calculators. The NACA became NASA (the National Aeronautics and Space Administration). Things changed for Katherine also. She and the other women involved in the new space program were expected to write new textbooks since there were none. The women in the program had to contend with on the job sexism. They were never allowed briefings or have their names on their research. When Katherine was promoted to aerospace technologist in 1958, she co-wrote twenty-eight research papers. Some of her work included charting the course for Alan Shepard's suborbital flight aboard Freedom 7 on May 5, 1961, John Glenn's orbital flight on February 20, 1962, and more challenging still, calculating the paths that Apollo 11 would take to and from the moon. In 2015, President Barack Obama bestowed the Presidential Medal of Freedom upon Katherine Johnson.

Paul R. Williams
Born: 1894
Died: 1980

PAUL R. WILLIAMS

Paul R. William's dream was to become an architect. It astonished him when his teacher acknowledged the fact that he had the ability, but advised him to pursue another profession. He was convinced that black architects needed white clients in order to succeed in that business. After thinking about it for a brief time, contrary to his teacher's advice, Williams decides to follow his dream. He felt that if he did let being black stalemate his chances then, he would develop the habit of being defeated. Williams went on with his education in the field he loved. When he graduated from Polytechnic High School in 1912 he continues to learn more about architecture. Within three years Williams went into business as a certified building contractor. He joined the Los Angeles Architectural Club to take advantage of the perks related to his business. A member could take classes and also enter competitions sponsored by the other clubs. He enrolled at the University of Southern California for three years. He left before graduating because of his need to work. Realizing his need for additional skills in technique, Williams took night and weekend courses at a few art schools where various techniques were taught. Now he was better prepared to enter and win competitions. And he did win some. Still studying, Williams began working at white-owned firms that specialized in landscape architecture, luxury homes, and, commercial buildings. His knowledge of physics and architectural engineering served him well. In 1921, nine years after he left high school, Paul R. Williams becomes a licensed architect. He opened his own business in LA's Stock Exchange Building. Initially, his projects were small ones that larger firms refused. He understood it was important to take the jobs that were available to him, big or small. Eventually, Williams attracted quite a few high-profile projects. That is not to say he never experience rejection because of race, he did. Things changed considerably for Williams in 1933. His stellar reputation as an architect paid off big for him. After the completion of his biggest project yet, a two-million-dollar showplace, Paul R. Williams' architectural skills were in demand. He was commissioned to design luxury homes in Beverly Hills, Bel Air and in other places by many of the celebrities in California. He designed or co-designed over twenty important commercial buildings in the Los Angeles area. Paul R. Williams worked on more than three thousand projects in the United States and abroad before retiring in the 1970s.

Mae Carol Jemison
Born: 1956

MAE CAROL JEMISON

Mae Jemison became the first African-American Woman to travel in space. She was born to Charlie and Dorothy Green Jemison on October 17, 1956 in Decatur, Alabama. Mae is the youngest of their three children. When Mae was three years old the Jemisons relocated to Chicago, Illinois in search of a better education for their children. In school Mae was a good student. She enjoyed reading books on astronomy and science fiction. Her family supported her scientific interests without reservations, but there were others who saw science as an unsuitable career for a woman. Nevertheless, it was the 1969 advent of Neil Armstrong, Michael Collins, and Edwin Aldrin's trip to the Moon on the Apollo II that really captured her attention. She researched as much as she could to find out more about the mission. When Mae entered high school, she had not lost her interest in science. She just had to decide which branch to pursue. Mae became interested in biomedical engineering. Though she participated in many other school activities, Mae kept her grades up. And after graduating high school at sixteen and winning a National Achievement Scholarship in 1973, she enters Stanford University in Palo Alto, California. She chose to major in chemical engineering and African-American studies. Mae had always done well in the science courses in high school, now she had to work harder than other students to be recognized by her science and engineering professors. Traditionally, engineering attracted males and not African-American females. In 1977, Mae Jemison graduated from Stanford University with a bachelor of science degree in chemical engineering and a bachelor of arts degree in African and African-American studies. Mae went to medical school at Cornell University until she developed an interest in internal medicine and left for Kenya in 1979. On her return in 1981, she graduated from medical school and finished her internship in 1982. From 1983 to 1985, Dr. Mae Jemison held the position as a staff doctor with the Peace Corps in West Africa. She managed health care for Peace Corps and U.S. embassy personnel and worked with the National Institutes of Health and the Centers for Disease Control. Dr. Jemison took part in several other important projects as well. With her mind still set on becoming an astronaut and traveling into space Dr. Jemison applied to the National Aeronautics and Space Administration (NASA). In October 1986 she was one of fifteen accepted out of two thousand applicants. After completing the yearlong intensive training, Dr. Jemison's long-awaited space flight came in 1992 on the space shuttle Endeavor.

Louis Daniel Armstrong
Born: 1901
Died: 1971

LOUIS DANIEL ARMSTRONG

    Louis Armstrong became America's most innovative trumpet player, known for revolutionizing jazz. His life began in the ghetto of New Orleans, Louisiana on August 4, 1901. His parents divorced when he was quite young. With little schooling he was destined for trouble, which he found on New Year's Day after firing a firearm into the air. Twelve years old Armstrong was taken to a boy's correction facility that changed the direction of his life. While at the facility he was fortunate to meet Peter Davis, a cornet player who taught him to play the instrument. After the boy's release three years later, he also learned to play a trumpet from popular jazz musician Joe "King" Oliver and then became his back-up until 1919. In 1924 Armstrong's popularity grew rapidly after joining Fletcher Henderson's famous African-American band in New York City. Audiences were thrilled by his unique timbre, rhythm, and style. During that time he also cut jazz records with the accomplished saxophonist Sidney Bechet. In 1925 after returning to Chicago Armstrong formed his own band called the "Hot Five" and later, the "Hot Seven", a move that changed jazz history. He changed the role of the soloist, to be the focal point of any jazz performance or recording. Recorded examples of the change he made are in, "Muskrat Ramble", "Muggles" "Cornet Chop Suey", and "Potato Head Blues". Armstrong is given credit for initiating scat singing and naturally imitating the sounds of horns. His music was well received in the States as well as internationally. He was given the nickname "Satchel-mouth" and later "Satchmo", and referred to as "The Master of Good Will" because of the effect he had on audiences. Armstrong gained his fan's respect not only for being a masterful musician, but his personality and his musical definition of the black American soul. And later, songs like "(What Did I Do To Be So) Black And Blue" and "I Can't Give You Anything But Love" gained even more recognition for the trumpet player. His singing "Ain't Misbehavin'" from the orchestra pit of the Broadway show, Hot Chocolates, launched his career onto the stage and more in the public eye during the 1930s and 1940s. Though he appeared in over fifty films, he continued to perform in serious jazz concerts with fellow musicians. It is said the whole of jazz music was transformed by the genius of Armstrong. He had nineteen top ten records. Armstrong died on July 6, 1971 at the age of 69 in Corona, Queens, New York.

Barbara Charlaine Jordan
Born: 1936
Died: 1996

BARBARA CHARLAINE JORDAN

Barbara Jordan was the first black woman from the South elected to the U.S. Congress. A follower in the tradition of Thurgood Marshall, Jordan was a champion of civil rights and an opponent of political corruption. Jordan never hesitated to speak boldly upon the issues of social injustice and constitutional integrity. She spoke on a range of difficult issues from the Watergate scandal to the North American Free Trade Agreement with the same fervor. Barbara Jordan was born February 21, 1936 to Benjamin and Arlyne Patton Jordan. During her schools' years she showed exceptional talent debating for which she received many awards. In 1952 to 1956 Jordan entered Texas State University to do undergraduate work under Professor Thomas Freedman, her mentor. She became part of his debating team that was the first debate team from a black university to compete in a law tournament held annually at Baylor University in Texas. Jordan did not disappoint, she won first place in junior oratory. Jordan graduated magna cum laude from Texas Southern University in 1956. And she received a law degree in 1959 from Boston University. After moving back to Texas to start a law practice, Jordan got involved with the civil rights movement. Eventually, her interest in politics grew so strong she launched a campaign to run for the Texas State House of Representatives in 1962. Losing did not deter her spirit in the least. In 1966, Jordan employed the protest tactics that voting rights groups used to get the Voting Rights Act of 1965 signed by President Lyndon Johnson. She won this time becoming the first African-American woman to be elected to the Texas State Senate. Jordan's years as a senator brought about many positive changes. Barbara Jordan became famous for interpreting the Constitution for the people of her state. Aware that the Texas restrictive voter registration law affected Mexican-Americans and blacks most of all, Jordan established The Texas Department of Community Affairs. She was responsible for creating a Texas Fair Employment Practices Commission to improve workmen's compensation and to set a minimum wage for the poor and the farm workers. In 1972, Jordan was elected to the Congress. As a junior member of the judiciary committee in the House she took part in the impeachment hearings of Richard Nixon. After Jordan is stricken with multiple sclerosis she retires from the political arena in 1978 to teach law at the University of Texas. The Presidential Medal of Freedom was bestowed on her by President Bill Clinton in 1994.

John H. Johnson
Born: 1918
Died: 2005

JOHN H. JOHNSON

John H. Johnson, publisher of Ebony and Jet magazines became the wealthiest black business man in the 1940s and 1950s. He was born into poverty to a mother whose schooling ended in third grade. She wanted more for her child. When her husband died the boy was only six. But after eighth grade she moved him to Chicago in 1933 seeking a better education. There was no high school in her home town of Arkansas for black students. Johnson entered Du Sable High School known for its very high standards. He studied hard and graduated with distinction in 1936. Johnson helped the family with finances during the depression, so he took a job opportunity and training offered to high school and college students. Though he earns a scholarship to attend the University of Chicago, he did not finish his studies there. He accepted a part time job with Supreme Life Insurance Company while attending Northwestern University School of Commerce. The Company was so impressed with his work he was given a full-time job as editor of their company journal. Part of his job was to make lists of articles that might interest black readers to include in the journal. He got the idea of publishing a black magazine, "The Negro Digest" in 1942. The goal was to bring about interracial understanding and national unity. The magazine was so well received, its circulation reached 50,000 in a short time. That initial success led to the publishing of Ebony Magazine which turned out to be even more popular than the first. The first issue came out in November of 1945. It examined racial issues, civil rights legislation, and black family life. It also told about social success, and black economics. In 1951, Jet magazine hit the news stand. It was quite popular, but not to the same degree as Ebony. Johnson built an empire that expanded into countless other successful business ventures. He was the first African American to appear on Forbes magazine's list of the four hundred wealthiest Americans. In 1966, Johnson was awarded the Spingarn Medal by the NAACP, for his contributions to Africa American Culture.

Wilt Chamberlain
Born: 1936
Died: 1999

WILT CHAMBERLAIN

Wilt Chamberlain was born Wilton Norman Chamberlain on August 21, 1936. He was one of nine siblings raised in Philadelphia, Pennsylvania. His mother Olivia was a domestic worker and his father William was a welder and a custodian. During the boy's earlier years, he was quite sickly, often missing many days from school. Always tall for his age he was called "Wilt the Stilt" because of his 7 feet 1-inch height. In high school Chamberlain was an outstanding athlete in several sports, track and field, football, and baseball included. His summer vacations were spent working as a bellhop in a city hotel. While in high school he refused every offer extended to get him to join one of their professional teams. His goal was to attend college, and that he did. The University of Kansas was his choice. He led the Jayhawks, the university's team to the national college finals. Leaving before senior year, Chamberlain signed up with the popular professional team, the Harlem Globetrotters. Wilt Chamberlain signed up to play on the Philadelphia Warriors team in 1959. He became the first basketball player to ever score 100 points in a single game (1961--1962) season. He later was traded to the Philadelphia 76ers. He led them to a victorious championship (1966--1967) season. Chamberlain also became the first player in the National Basketball Association to score a total of 30,000 points. He set that record in 1972 while still playing for the Los Angeles Lakers. After a brief stint (1973--1974) as coach for the San Diego Conquistadors he then retired from the game to pursue other business and entertainment ventures. One venture in particular became his passion, volleyball. In 1974, Chamberlain became a board member of the newly formed International Volleyball Association and shortly after, its president. He was named to the Volleyball Hall of Fame. Before his death his careers highlights and awards were many. Wilt Chamberlain died in BelAir, California on October 12, 1999 at the age of 63.

Alex Haley
Born: 1921
Died: 1992

ALEX HALEY

 Alex Haley was an African American writer who had a very personal story to share. He went to great lengths to validate it as truth. His family elders told stories of their ancestral past when he and his brothers came to visit from Ithaca, New York. He watched as his grandmother sat on her porch in Henning, Tennessee bobbing her head in agreement. The stories she said had been passed on from generation to generation since the time of slavery. Certain details stayed with Haley as grew up. As a young man Alex Haley joined the Coast Guard and spent seventeen years at sea. He began to write for the Coast Guard newspaper. After leaving the Coast Guard and settling in New York, he continued writing. It was not until after he had written, "The Autobiography of Malcolm X" in 1965 he began to think about researching his own family ancestral history. Haley was so inspired by the success of the autobiography, he decided to visit the National Archives building in Washington, D.C. where all family records in the United States are stored. From the family stories he recalled the mentioning of a man called "the African." After searching the 1870 records he found the names of his great-grandparents and eventually the one called "the African." He remembered hearing that the man was captured in Africa by slave traders and forced aboard a slave ship bound for a place called "Napolis" in America. Haley also recalled that the family said, on the ship "the African" insisted on being called "Kin-tay." After meeting with an African language expert, the writer was sent to Gambia where the Kinte family was well known. There he heard an account of 17-year-old Kunta Kinte's kidnapping in the year 1765. It took Alex Haley twelve years to follow all the leads and do the research required to have his story come together. Haley put all the facts in his book called, Roots that he published in 1976. Though it is a story written about the ancestral family of Alex Haley, it is the story of black people everywhere. It became a very popular television mini-series that first aired in 1977. Alex Haley died in 1992.

Patricia Bath
Born: 1942

PATRICIA BATH

Patricia Bath showed great interest in science and mathematics very early. In school she excelled in both subjects and was encouraged to pursue a career in science by her teachers. During her years in high school Bath spent a great deal of time helping in biology lab in order to learn more about the science. Her willingness to work hard resulted in her receiving numerous awards in science. A greater pay off came when she was chosen to participate in a National Science Foundation Summer program for high school students at Yeshiva University. Following high school, Bath got a job working at Yeshiva University and Harlem Hospital with the cancer research team of Rabbi Moses D. Tendler and Dr. Robert O. Bernard, also her mentors. She proved to be a real asset to the team. Her job was to collect and analyze experimental data, develop a hypothesis, and develop a mathematic equation to predict cancer cell growth. Bath's contribution to the research team was so valuable she was given credit as a co-author on the research report presented at the Fifth Annual International Congress on Nutrition in Washington, D.C. on September 2, 1960. At seventeen, she saw this as an important step toward a future in medicine. Her enrollment at Hunter College in New York was a great experience for her. She made the dean's list consistently. Bath received a bachelor of arts degree in chemistry with highest honors in 1964. She entered Howard Medical School with the same fervor. At the school she received many scholarships and awards, including the National Institute of Health Fellowship and the National Institute of Mental Health Fellowship in 1965. After spending a summer doing health research of children in Yugoslavia, Bath developed an interest in international medicine. Her desire to help the disadvantaged, moved her to become coordinator for the Poor People's Campaign that marched for economic rights in Washington, D.C. in 1968. Completing medical school in that same year, Dr. Bath trained in ophthalmology (the study of the human eye) and also worked as an assistant of surgery at several hospitals until moving to California. She continued her work at the UCLA Medical Center, later becoming its first Black female surgeon. After serving as chief of Ophthalmology in Nigeria, Africa for a year, Dr. Bath went to Berlin University in Germany to do further research. After her return to the U.S. Dr. Bath invented a laser device for removing cataracts, (an ailment that affects the eye). Dr. Patricia Bath became the first African American female doctor to receive a patent for a medical invention.

Hattie McDaniel
Born: 1895
Died: 1952

HATTIE MCDANIEL

    Hattie McDaniel was an early African American radio personality. She was born June 10, 1895 in Wichita, Kansas to Henry McDaniel and Susan Holbert, former slaves. She was the youngest of their thirteen children. The family eventually moved to Denver, Colorado where Hattie graduated from high school. Much later she became a Hollywood actress and appeared in over three hundred films. She is especially remembered for her role as Mammy in the movie Gone with the Wind. She won an Academy Award for Best Supporting Actress in 1939. Hattie was not the only performer in the family. She had brothers and a sister in show business also. Sometimes Hattie sang with one brother's minstrel show. After his death in 1916, Hattie got little work except for touring with a black ensemble. In mid-1920's she began singing on the radio in Denver and making recordings for companies in other cities. From the many recordings, only four were ever issued. In 1929, Hattie could only find work as a washroom attendant or waitress because of the stock market crash. At the club where she worked the owner gave her a chance to perform on stage. After that, she became a regular. In 1931, Hattie moved to Los Angeles to live with her brother Sam and sisters Etta and Orlena. Sam got her a job at the radio station where he worked. Though her show became popular, her salary was so meager she still had to work as a maid. Her biggest breaks came after she joined the Screen Actors Guild in 1934. She landed major roles which won her screen credits. Large companies like Fox Film Corporation signed her under their contract. Hattie worked with celebrities and became friends with many. As her fame grew she received much criticism from some of the black community for the parts that she accepted. They felt stereotypes portrayed by her characterization were making it difficult for blacks to overcome racism and succeed. It is said her retort was "It is better to play a maid than to be one". Hattie McDaniel was the first African American to win an Oscar. In 1975 she was inducted into the Black Filmmakers Hall of Fame. She died on October 26, 1952.

William Grant Still
Born: 1895
Died: 1978

WILLIAM GRANT STILL

William Grant Still became the first African American to conduct a major symphony orchestra. He was born in Mississippi in 1895, but when his father died, his mother and he moved to Little Rock, Arkansas. His mother Carrie, a high school teacher, met and married his stepfather Charles Shepperson. Charles encouraged his stepson William's musical interests by exposing him to operettas and buying him various classical recordings, and even attending some performances by musicians on tour. The boy loved it all. At fifteen, William taught himself to play a few different instruments as his love for music grew. When he graduated from high school at sixteen, his mother wanted him to attend medical school, so William pursued a Bachelor of Science degree program at Wilberforce University in Ohio. While at the school William became a member of Kappa Alpha Psi fraternity. He conducted the university band, learned to play instruments, and started to compose and to do orchestrations. He was awarded scholarships to study at the Oberlin Conservatory of Music with Friedrick Lehmann and George Whitefield Chadwick. He also studied with Edgard Varese later. When World War I started Williams joined the United States Navy. After leaving the Service, he worked as an arranger for some of the popular bands of the 1920s. In the 1930s, Still worked as an arranger of popular music for NBC Radio Broadcasts while composing concert picces, using the influences of African American music: spirituals, blues, and jazz. Then in 1931, the Rochester Philharmonic performed his Afro-American Symphony. It was the first time a symphony orchestra had performed a work by an African-American composer. In 1936, Still conducted the Los Angeles Philharmonic Orchestra; he was the first African American to conduct a major American orchestra. And in 1949, Still's opera, Troubled Island was performed by a leading opera company, the New York City Opera, another first for Still. William Still composed more than 150 works, including, five symphonies and eight operas before his death on December 3, 1978.

Lawrence Douglas Wilder
Born: 1931

LAWRENCE DOUGLAS WILDER

Lawrence Wilder became the first African American to be elected Governor in the United States. He was born in Richmond, Virginia January 17, 1931 to Beulah Olive and Robert Judson Wilder. He was one of eight siblings. His parents named him after two famous men, Frederick Douglas, once a slave turned freedom fighter, and Paul Laurence Dunbar, a black poet. Living through the Depression even though his family was poor, they did not think of themselves as destitute. Upon entering Virginia Union University, he had to support himself by working in a hotel waiting tables and shining shoes. Wilder received a degree in chemistry from the University in 1951. After being drafted in the Army during the Korean War, he chose combat duty and subsequently was awarded the Bronze Star Medal for heroism. When Wilder was discharge from the Army in 1953 he had made Sergeant. Once at home he worked in the state medical examiner's office while he pursued a master's degree in chemistry. His plans changed in 1956 when he decided to study law. He left home to do so. By law African Americans were not allowed to enroll in Virginia law schools. Wilder enrolled at Howard University School of Law in Washington, D.C. in 1956. After receiving a law degree in 1959, Wilder set up a law practice in Richmond, Virginia. He worked just as hard for the poor as he did for those who had means. He entered the political arena in 1969 and was elected Virginia's first African American state senator since Reconstruction. He waged a battle to end racial discrimination in housing and jobs, and to create a state holiday to honor Dr. Martin Luther King, Jr. Lawrence Wilder made history when he was elected to be his state's first African America lieutenant governor in 1985, and four years later elected governor. During his tenure as Governor he dealt with such pressing issues as crime and gun control, carrying out Virginia's laws on capital punishment, etc. In recognition of such an achievement, the NAACP awarded him the Spingarn Medal for 1990.

Lloyd Augustus Hall
Born: 1894
Died: 1971

LLOYD AUGUSTUS HALL

Lloyd Hall is remembered for his discovery of alternative ways to keep food fresh for longer periods of time. He devoted a great deal of his effort to researching the feasibility of preserving certain foods, especially meats. He also investigated the role that certain spices played in food preservation. Hall was born on June 19, 1894 in Elgin, Illinois to Augustus and Isabell Hall. Much later the family moved to Aurora, Illinois where he graduated from Eastside High School in 1912. Then Hall attended Northwestern University where he studied pharmaceutical chemistry. After earning a B.S. degree, Hall enrolled at the University of Chicago where he received a Master's degree. Afterwards he applied for a position with the Western Electric Company. Unfortunately, at the actual interview, Hall was rejected because of his race. He then obtained employment with the Department of Health in Chicago until an opening came available with the John Morrell Company. He was hired as the company's chief chemist. However, Lloyd Hall's chemist career with the Morrell Company was prematurely interrupted by World War I. He served with the United States Ordinance Department as Chief Inspector of powder and explosives. At the end of his tour, Hall married and returned to Chicago to continue the work that he left. This time he became President and Chemical director for Chemical Products Corporation's consulting laboratory. In 1925, Hall was asked to take a position with the Griffith Laboratories. And that he did. Hall's discovery of chemicals and treatments to keep food fresh longer was certainly a benefit. During World War II his methods were very important to the U.S. Military. The food supply for their troops stayed safe and lasted longer without spoilage. He also devised a new technique to kill bacteria that cause diseases. It is still used to sterilize bandages in hospitals today. He received fifty-nine patents in the United States and a number his inventions were patented in foreign countries. The scientist stayed with Griffith Laboratories until his retirement in 1959. In his lifetime he received several awards for his many contributions. Lloyd Augustus Hall died in 1971.

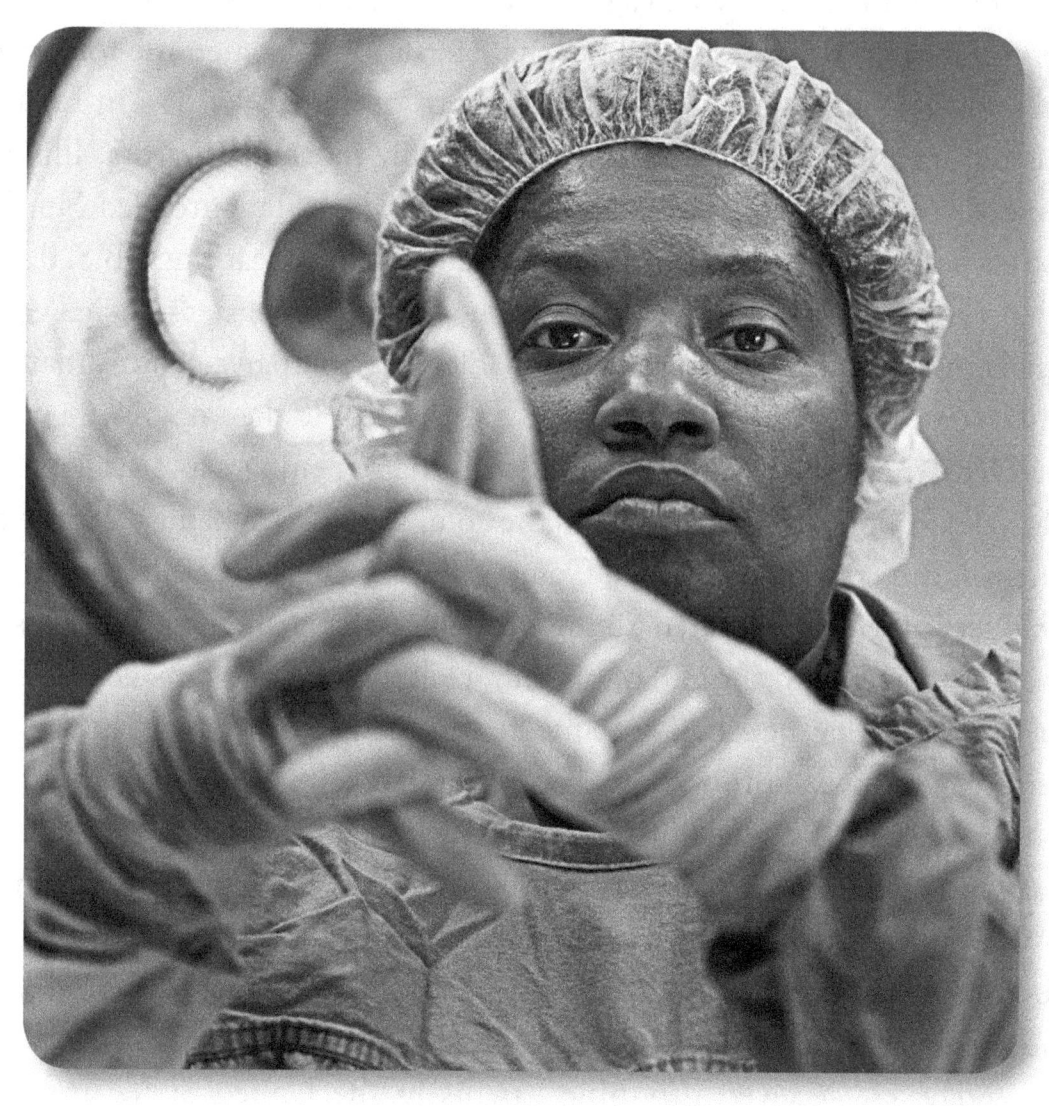

Alexa Canady
Born: 1950

68 | BARBARA A. PIERCE

ALEXA CANADY

Alexa Canady was the first African American female neurosurgeon in the United States. She was born on November 7, 1950 in a rural area outside Lansing, Michigan. Her father Clinton Canady was a dentist, and her mother Hortense Golden Canady was a homemaker. Alexa was the most inquisitive of their four children. Her parents encouraged it, and made sure all of their children were exposed to books, cultural events and travel. Alexa was an excellent student in all of her classes. There was an incident questioning Alexa's academic ability after doing better on an exam than her second-grade classmates. Her teacher could not accept the fact that the only African American child in her class could possibly be smarter than her white students. Her refusal to give the grade Alexa had earned, caused her to be terminated after the situation was investigated. That was the child's first experience with racism. In high school Alexa did so well she graduated with highest honors in 1967. She then entered the University of Michigan where she participated on their debating team and was a journalist for the student newspaper. Her initial plan of being a theoretical mathematician changed when she realized mathematics was not her niche. Alexa then received a bachelor of science degree. After spending a summer working in a minority health care program working with a pediatrician and geneticist, her interest switched to medicine. Alexa completed her medical studies at the University at Michigan with a specialty in pediatric neurosurgery in which she proved to be an outstanding student. In 1975 Dr. Alexa Canady received her degree and a citation from the American Medical Women's Association. And after working at various hospitals she was certified by the American Board of Neurological Surgery in 1984. It seems that Dr. Alexa Canady finally found her niche when she chose to go into medicine. She became chief of neurosurgery at Children's Hospital in Detroit, Michigan.

BIBLIOGRAPHY

Becker, Chrisanne. 100 African Americans Who Changed American History. World Almanac Library. Milwaukee, WI. 2005.

Boden, Pathfinders: The Journey of 16 Extraordinary Black Souls. Abrams Books for young readers. New York, NY. 2017.

Estell, Kenneth, et. al. African-American Portrait of a People. Visible Ink Press, a Division of Gale Research Inc. Detroit, Michigan. 1994.

Falstein, Mark. Meeting the Challenge: Biographies of Black Americans. The Continental Press, Inc. Elizabethtown, Pennsylvania. 1987.

Gates, Jr. Henry Louis, et al. The African-American Century: How Black Americans Have Shaped Our Country. Simon and Schuster. New York, N.Y. 2002.

Gates, Jr. Henry Louis. Life Upon These Shores: Looking At African American History 1513---2008. Alfred A. Knopf, a division of Random House, Inc. New York and Canada. 2011.

Hayden, Robert C. Achievers: African-Americans in Science and Technology: 9 African-American Inventors. Twenty-First Century Books, a Division of Henry Holt and Company, Inc. New York, N.Y. 1992.

Jackson, Tricia Williams. Women in Black History: Stories of Courage, Faith, and Resilience. Revell: A Division of Baker Publishing Group. Grand Rapids, Michigan. 2016.

Lanker, Brain. I Dream A World: Portraits of Black Women Who Changed America. Stewart, Tabor and Chang. New York, N.Y. 1999.

McNair, Joseph D. Barbara Jordan African American Politician. The Child's World, Inc. Chanhassen, MN. 2001.

Potter, Joan, et. al. African Americans Who Were First. Cobblehill Books, a division of Penguin Books USA, Inc. New York, N.Y. 1997.

Schraff, Anne. American Heroes of Exploration and Flight. Enslow Publishers, Inc. Berkeley Heights, New Jersey. 1996.

Sullivan, Otha Richard. Black Stars: African American Inventors. John Wiley and Sons, Inc. New York, N.Y. 1998.

Sullivan, Otha Richard. Black Stars: African American Women Scientists and Inventors. John Wiley and Sons, Inc. New York, N.Y. 2002.

Yanauzzi, Della A. Mae Jemison: A Space Biography. Enslow Publishers, Inc. Springfield, New Jersey. 1998.

ADDITIONAL RESEARCH RECOMMENDATIONS

Writers
Toni Morrison
Gwendolyn Brooks
Maya Angelou

Politics
Carol Moseley-Braun
Adam Clayton Powel
Bill Gray
Ronald Brown

Medicine/ Math/ Science
Jane Cook Wright
Betty Wright Harris
Marjorie Lee Brown
Shirley Ann Jackson
Valerie Thomas
Robert E. Shurney

Sports
Satchel Paige
Carl Lewis
Jack Johnson
Jackie Joyner-Kersee
Alice Coachman

Law
Pamela Carter

Military
Colin Powell
Daniel "Chappie" James, Jr.

Historian
Lerone Bennett, Jr.

Media Producer/Actress/Humanitarian
Oprah Winfrey

www.ingramcontent.com/pod-product-compliance
Lightning Source LLC
Chambersburg PA
CBHW081506070526
44586CB00019B/2492